Variations in an Emergency

poems by

Anne Lovering Rounds

Variations in an Emergency is the 2014 winner of the Cathlamet Prize for Poetry.

Acknowledgments: The following were originally published in the following and are reprinted by permission: "Orpheus epilogue": *Penny Ante Feud* 16 (Spring 2015); "Practice," "Gradual": *Hartskill Review* 1.1 (Spring 2014); "Orpheus redux": *New Writing* 11.1 (January 2014); "Flight," "Blink": *Coldnoon* 2.4 (September 2013). This publication was subsidized in part by Harvard Studies in Comparative Literature.

Cover: Robert Motherwell, Untitled from the series Lyric Suite (April-May 1965). Brush and ink on Japanese mulberry paper. Gift of the artist to the Museum of Modern Art in memory of Frank O'Hara. Cover art © Dedalus Foundation/ Licensed by VAGA, New York, NY.

ISBN: 978-0-9905265-6-8

FIRST EDITION

Published by:
Ravenna Press
www.ravennapress.com

Table of contents

Variations in an Emergency

Aria

(Not for Frank O'Hara)

Running that night last august the red bridge
over the charles after falling

in love again
we'd talked about crane
dear heart how like you this
dear hart how like you

it's too fast on the express
I took the journey out of order
of someone who had hart's eyes I guess

cheers you said
what would our renaissance have been

Ann Arbor variation

On the *polterabend*, humid August night
I play the first dance in the second book
on my ex's Petrof. Schumann marked it

balladenmäßig, sehr rasch
as if I wouldn't give everything
to have one more second

to tell you *listen to this*

we thought we wanted to get out
of this town, forsake our ghosts

but even in midtown
someone has to clear the leaves
which you know always come

Meditation on an Emergency

Inside the tranquil bubble
of a northbound M1 and
by the distracting pastoral
of a fountain in midtown
I only idly long for a chaser
to what you never told me straight before

last week I was Florestan
today Eusebius

Meditation on an Emergency II

Last night in the Bronx a jackknifed truck
missed me in its sightline as it slipped
downhill faster and faster. Even before,
already late, I'd panicked, couldn't tell
the route that seemed familiar, couldn't tell
my parents anything: *I'm supposed to be*
in class or *wait* or *this is it.* As
the truck bore down I woke
remembering a dream two nights before,
equally implausible, another textbook
crush: your arms jackknifed around me,
nowhere except there I had to be.

Passage

Our Latin teacher scorned second and third looks
how many times can you re-read she said

I come back now to passages we'd done
knowing the change after ten years away

how the soil crumbled in my hand
how the light fell at Baiae

For my student

What he said
the last time
I saw him

they told me
I had a stroke

imagine a string
pulling you to the ceiling

one day I'll look up and it won't be there

Practice

Pain science isn't well understood, the physical
therapist said, *you probably felt better*
because you were focusing on something else.
Some people come in here with terrible
problems. What the fuck. I'd rather
do this alone anyway, as ritual, stretch
a band of invisible fascia, pull fifteen times
against tension, an enigma, do the work
to make the key strike the hammer strike
the string.

Out

mission
west portal
embarcadero

you are not here, not in the cruel
morphologies of *battery*, *chambers*, *wall*

at the end the blustery edge
of this island

Did you feel it

asked everybody
before we all
went to see
if we were all right

and check online if
it was a five point three
or a five point five

and in the popout chat window
I said nobody needed to evacuate

down here and the half-finished tower
looks the same as yesterday

From page proofs fucked up by Copier B

primary questions

under Grant Number 0213959

identities remain

enterprise may affect all relationships

    lying process.

"it is not so much

A prominent item on the political agenda in 2001 was

the amended version of the Securing America

even more prominent after September

, italics added)

the origins of perceptions

that together the happiness has been doubled

Liberty Island

Twice we undress,
place all items on a belt.
We're both asked for ID.
I touch the screen,
give away my fingerprint
for a locker. *Verified. Confirmed.*
Please insert $1 to leave behind
all your belongings except
one camera, any medicine.
Where are you from,
the guard asks. *We're from here.*

Gradual

Even when it's built
the tower will never be
finished

people do crazy shit there,
our friend said, one woman
threw a Subway sandwich
into one of the pools, and

each night, my wife, a bronzeworker,
rubs the graffiti names out of the plaque

a gradual reverse epigraphy

Blink

Two three red in a black tunnel

instead of the endgame

meditate on the idea of 32

blank paper

field of snow

flashback

Columbus Circle, was it? Ninetysixth?

Dear Christopher

at 96th street they rigged

the double concerto, one player on each

platform did you hear it

beautiful name close canon

Christopher I missed

Phase music variation

two loops two trains

b d f v when did I stop

playing the typewriter if

I am not playing how

will I keep you

Dream After Taking the Q64

The dream didn't make clear it was Jewel Ave,
the dark wide road the bus had traveled down
the night before, but I know it was. On this road I tried
my key in a lockbox: the one at Ridgewood Savings Bank,
maybe; or the bank of mailboxes on Morton Street
where my duplicate key always sticks; or the casket
they closed as everyone turned away. Traditionally
Chinese don't look, a gesture of respect, but the dream
was a form of looking: remembering red envelopes we got
as wedding gifts, the gold you and your children gave,
jewels saved and yet respent, passed down
along familiar open avenues.

Wie aus der Ferne

I was the last to leave the lecture hall.

In the dream I looked like a stereotype

of a professor, too much stuff,

two messenger bags and a copy of Auden's

light verse. As we left you held the door

for me, offered to carry everything,

though I declined. You kept on ahead

but turned around

in front of Memorial Church and said

you were going to get some lunch, to have a drink

and would I like to come, and should you bring

your car around,

a conversation that we never had in life.

I wish I had said yes, had called you back

before I realized, waking, dreaming already had.

Deadlift

Why is this difficult? Yes, it's a miracle
we manage to bear anything
at all. My piano teacher said
to seek out austere, joyless music,
which is meet and right: for even if
poetry is the spontaneous overflow
of powerful feelings I lift my spirits
by removing myself, raising a glass
to the dead who lift us.

Flight

Waiting, there's only the fadeout
of what was on the platform,
canals and outlines, the two three
suspension in an Ives quartet. The train's coming

flash forward to the tarmac, JFK,
the open timespan before takeoff
infinity in a runway queue
before we evaporate
into the sky, resolve suspense,
and disappear from view.

Tag

A hallucination in 98-degree
heat an epigraph inscribed
into the toxic monochrome
a white chalk blur along
the BQE when lilacs last
in the dooryard bloomed

M86

Dip your card into the slot,
even in the middle of the day
the M86 is full, each April
a catalogue of past Aprils:
there will always be another
ode to the crosstown

Giving blood

Phrases hang too long here in the air

you okay
halfway there

how you doing
relax

I empty and double myself
and staring up imagine purgatory

as a makeshift space just like this one
where, drained, you ask if you can go

they won't hold you hostage no more

Amadeus

After Newtown I remembered my father
standing at the pauper's grave in Wien

so much to give, he didn't say
so much that could have been

Little Lennon elegy

downtown someone is always
wearing glasses
walking on carmine

would this be you at fifty

to not know this
is like woolworth apex
invisible in cloud

Childhood variation

You were premature
we didn't know
if you would make it

a suite is music
no one was sure
would make it

A true account of waiting for a call from Merrill Lynch

James described the home as *broken*,
described his retrospect
as *the smoked glass of being thirty-six*,
described each avocado he had coaxed
to grow, alone, in water.

I imagine we'll discuss my age
and strategize the future. Thinking
of the vows, I'll say *Let me jump*
into the dark pool. You'll say it depends
exactly how much risk you want to take.

Golden Gate

The bridge makes an impression by being obscured
as we walk through the parkland in the chill
night cloud, laughing at our party clothes

we hold each other's hand, predict
the foghorn interval

orient ourselves
in this minor third

this bridge we know
icon we do not see

Anniversary

After it was over, the toasts, the dance, the cake,

still half too drunk to play the day's reel back,

alone we checked our email. You hadn't been

home long, you wrote, but were recovering fine,

sending best wishes, open, eloquent,

maybe high post-op; then the money line,

will you preach my funeral. How you knew,

not only how to ask, but how to teach

by asking: teach me to take

the vows again, each time to say

yes. Of course for you I will.

Orpheus redux

Late at night, Broadway at twenty-third
I ran and ran and ran, streets tumbling
away as each light turned,
a blur, and crossing Union Square

the tension in your face
came back to me, the moment that you said
in passing that your friend was struck and killed
crossing this street. For a second

you could have lost it and I wish
I'd touched your hand,
known what to say, just as

when yesterday I saw my student slip
away from me in class, I wanted
so much to stop it from happening;
instead, as each new sentence tumbled out
he drifted further and further.

An awkward date, October '99.
We were running late,
the freeway tangled as we reached Detroit.
I forgot the program that we heard,
except that there was Bach,
and what Sam said
when we had caught our breath:

all I had to hear was those few notes;
it was as if
none of it had happened,
everything fell
away.

Orpheus epilogue

Orpheus had it figured out:
we're always losing each other
by accident, looking back
or pressing too hard and

what will mitigate but not reverse this loss
is a sequence in the third movement
of the Italian Concerto I didn't even
remember was there until it happened

Hommage à R. Sch.

Like you I love
to repeat slash
extend the end
we know is
coming. Is this it.
Is it. No it's
this.

Aria

take the repeat

we were never here

About the author

Anne Lovering Rounds is an assistant professor of English at Eugenio María de Hostos Community College, a campus of the City University of New York located in the South Bronx. A native of Ann Arbor, Michigan, she graduated from the University of Chicago with degrees in English and Classics (2004) and holds a doctorate in Comparative Literature from Harvard (2009). Her work has appeared in journals including *Coldnoon*, *Hartskill Review*, *Literary Imagination*, *New Writing*, *Penny Ante Feud*, and *Proteus*. As a pianist, she has studied with teachers including Gurminder Bhogal, Teresa Dybvig, Jeffers Engelhardt, Ruth Rose, Adam Tendler, and Sarah Trinkaus. This is her first book.